STARLAND

Jessica Purdy

Nixes Mate Books
Allston, Massachusetts

Copyright © 2017 Jessica Purdy

Book design by d'Entremont
Cover photograph by Fabrice Poussin

All rights reserved. This book or any portion thereof may not be reproduced or used in any manner whatsoever without the express written permission of the publisher except for the use of brief quotations in a book review or scholarly journal.

ISBN 978-0-9991882-9-3

Nixes Mate Books
POBox 1179
Allston, MA 02134
nixesmate.pub/books

*For Paul, Jack, and Mae
and in memory of Joan*

Contents

After Rain	1
202 Bank Street, Harwich Port, Massachusetts	2
Mystery	4
After the Bookstore Reading	6
Accident	8
The Beekeeper's Daughter	10
After Watching Rosemary's Baby Again at 46	12
Martinizing Confession	14
November	15
The Myth of the Bumblebee	16
After a Long Winter	18
Beach Houses in Snow	19
My Son Says	20
Proof	22
Journey to the Underworld	24
Cape Cod, Massachusetts	26
A Harp Seal	28
Cold-Blooded	29
My Daughter Asks	30

What I Love About Dreams	32
The Mystery of Footprints	34
At the Dream Museum	36
Driving to Your Parents	38
Someone I Love Might Die	40
STARLAND	41
Night Walk While You are Dying	42
Amazing Story	44
News of the Missing Girl	45
Midsummer Murder Suicide	46
I dreamed that	48
Can You Hear Me?	49
Perennial as Love	50
Back of the Dance Class	52
Voice while Driving	53
The Poem She Never Wrote	54
Winter River	56
The Jar with the Dry Rim	57

STARLAND

After Rain

In the breeze of a sunny June morning
an undersea story emerges in the current.
The trees seem to wash like kelp beds
brindled green through the half-mist of distance
humid cool in the blue-shadowed bower
and nearby iris petals flutter like fish fins
their leaves glisten and flash with fallen stars –
and what of the hummingbird's sudden entrance,
the grace in her motionless motion?
Her iridescent hunger I want to cup in my hands
before she abruptly vanishes.
Why, in my contentment, do I still thirst
for other worlds, words for beauty that reveal
themselves as messages from the sea?

202 Bank Street, Harwich Port, Massachusetts

The green scent of mown lawn triggers
those childhood summers on Cape Cod
where, on the gravel patio, my mother
taught us how to make corn husk dolls
and toy sailboats out of wood and cloth.
Our red Sunfish, Tipsy, lay on one side
paint chipping in the sunny yard.

The house, a perfume of must and soap,
damp wood and linoleum, sounded
like squeaky drawers. An odd staircase
led up to a trapdoor into the cold
bathroom, our rocket ship pocket
of space that turned children spectral
in the dark on a humid midday.

Table Talk pies at the brown kitchen table
and my brother paining us; the dirt road
with puddles after rain; the pine knoll
at the end where we dug for pottery
and arrowheads…What I wanted to say
was that home is not only the melding
of grass, soap, and unnamed flowers,

but the taste of a crabapple, the chimney
passing through my bedroom, my mother's
pen on damp paper, the sheets cooling
my sunburn, my skin burning the sheets –
a layering like the flayed flesh of that baby
rabbit our cat brought back alive.
Fur, then blood and bone.

How I longed to heal it, but could only visit
the box and surprise it with goodbye.

Mystery

I wanted to be a detective, a private eye.
I would lie on the blue corduroy
couch and read Nancy
Drew while nibbling on a cherry
chapstick. I wore a costume jewelry
emerald bracelet whose eye
shape affected me deeply
when it reflected the green light of day.
The idea of trapdoors consumed my
imagination. I wanted a secret staircase, a spy
code, a hiding place beneath a crumbly
board, a box filled with spidery
handwriting found in a gully.
My sister loved paper dolls of famous royalty.
I envied her knowledge of fancy
beheaded women and their finery,
but their dresses dripped with dislocation. They
had nothing to do with me. Every
old thing I found was a clue, even if it was miscellany.
Once I spent the entirety
of an afternoon trespassing quietly
on the neighbor's abandoned property

where I pieced together a tragedy
of newspaper clippings, tools, insect shells, and toys,
certain I would uncover the truth. Mystery
where there was none. Bravery.
Evidence is objects in eternity.
Here is what you cannot know. Now solve for y.

After the Bookstore Reading
for Kate Greenstreet

A deer dies in your book that won't be read
until after an actual deer runs out in front of my car.

He sees movement and sees me see him
and his decision – quick silver – liquid bright
is in his brown (o love) eye

and I'm hammering the brakes to a cartoon stop
that sends your book and the contents
of my purse spilling onto the floor.

I roll down my window and tell him:
"Hey, what are you doing? Go home!"

He stares at me like he understands
that no one understands him,
as if he's some dog cocking his head
meeting my relieved eyes with his lost ones.

Later, when I see the written image of your dead deer
that had been there in the car with me the whole time,
I feel I must tell you

there are different kinds of loss, degrees of permanence.
And that now, every single time I pass that spot,
I slow down in anticipation.

Accident

For Mark DeCarteret

I come upon a scene in the dark on the road home
after feeding your cat as you recover.
A deer in the middle of the road looks as if it's resting
settling down to sleep maybe, but then I see the blood,
greasy as black oil in my headlights,

and a woman pulled over on her phone.
I stop and ask if she's all right
thinking she must be the one who hit the deer
but no, she's only the one calling the police

whoever did hit the deer is gone
and all the people and cars pulling over
are a microcosm of a world
that illuminates suffering and dying.

The blue lights come –
their order-inducing panic –
the officer steps out
draws his weapon,
says nothing.

I think he hates this
I can tell by the way
he aims, checks, aims again
so he won't miss and cause more pain.

I cover my ears and the shot
is nothing I can prepare for;
the deer's head simply drops hard
the plumes of breath that had been vapor
dissipate, dissolve into the air

like the cars and people who soon leave
the road in darkness
the culprit just one of the bad in all this good.

The Beekeeper's Daughter

My hands are in the sink with the dishes
soap suds fragrant, back hurting,
a chore that leads to looking
out the window into the neighbor's yard

where the young lady who lives next door
stands beneath the tree I love
that holds the birds I love, different species
with each season,

stands beneath the tree luxuriating
in the sensation of "washing" her arms
with green leaves she has picked.
Carefully she wipes her cheeks

smooths her arms in a pantomime of showering
with lather, an inward smile on her lips.
Her bespectacled face thinks she is alone.
Somewhere along the line something went wrong.

During her pregnancy, the beekeeper
might have sensed it, some internal sensation,
clock off, some asymmetry? Whatever it was
made her come out lagging behind the others

but here she is and I feel a protective urge
to warn her about poison ivy
but turn back to my own task
with the feeling I'm missing something

honey, smoke, the comb loaded with tongue-sweet
and venom a toxin that may be passed
through the bloodstream
swarm with furred winged buzz,
the dance of intelligent life forms
who can find their own way home.

After Watching Rosemary's Baby Again at 46

You go out into the October daylight, squint
at a man walking past who pauses on the sidewalk
after you leave your driveway.
In the rearview you catch him looking
at where you came from.
You make a mental note to defend yourself
before you enter your house again.
A hawk skids above the highway
pulls up to the curb of wind
that rushes through leaves whose loss
seem like a mistake.
Strangers in the supermarket peer at you
over meat sealed in shiny plastic.
Your mind makes these leaps:
the betrayal of Charles Grodin's Dr. Hill,
his strangely comedic, cunning sneer,
the husband who talks about raping
Rosemary while she was drugged
shrugging it off as "fun, in a necrophile sort of way",
her voice as fairy light as her body –
almost a child's still,
and so in love with the idea of a baby

that the devil's fingernail scratches don't hurt.
Some kind of hysteria her husband
calls it when she loses her mind.
This is the point when madness is more like real life.
How you would have screamed long before this outrage,
at least blinked when he insulted your haircut
or searched through the trash for your book
on witchcraft he threw away.
If you remade that movie today
Rosemary would take that blade
and drive it into every one of those witches' skulls
and baby Satan too would be powerless against you.
Or would it happen the exact same way as in 1966
before you were even born and God was already dead?

Martinizing Confession
for Kate Greenstreet

When I was in high school I worked at a dry cleaners. I stabbed the labels of shirts and sweaters with a tagger and hung the clothes on a huge rack that ran all the way to the back. Covered with plastic, the clothes hung, bereft of warmth. Their owners would line up to retrieve them. One sweater stayed for a long time. It was ivory white, and soft, with a rolled collar I fingered with longing. I felt sad for it. The more time passed, the more I was justified in taking it. By summer, I figured someone had truly forgotten about its existence. I stole it, waited a few months, then began wearing it in the cooler days of fall. I rode around town not knowing who would recognize me, whether I was wearing it or not.

November

The days seem to be ending
even as they begin –
do you know what I mean,
when you're driving and the sun hacks

through leafless trunks
their shadows seem like an attack
or does the light
just hit the eye at the most defenseless angle

aggressive yellow not just a color but an ending
indicator, a preliminary warning
not of caution so much
as an obligatory direness, tired as a fist held too long

not warm as in goldleaf,
honey or even the cold daffodils of last spring
and after defending against such glare
the loneliest feeling comes?

The Myth of the Bumblebee
— bumblebees cannot fly, according to conventional aerodynamics

The bumblebees I saw asleep
in torpid suspended animation
this morning had been frozen
by the night frost half stuck
still sucking from the cups
of blossoms turned to humble
makeshift beds (other insects too,
menacing looking but still
in their bodies that never seem to decay
after death) then later reanimate
and begin their job where they left off
having stayed late to work finishing
the last of their rounds after leaving
the nest due to their maleness, not fed
but foraging for themselves and mating,
not workers for the colony who,
in the ground nest fashioned
from an old mouse house,
spit the nectar and feed the instars
future males or queens or workers;

does the queen mock the late all nighters in their cups
her honey pot filled for the harder days of weather;
they're aposematic and so, safe,
in their vulnerable slumber,
with their stingers that won't be suicide to wield
(but nearby a funnel web spider
is juicing perhaps even the bee's own brother)
later he flies – I saw it with my own eyes –
around the corollas having sufficiently
warmed his body to achieve the clap-fling
flight, the wingbeat biologists said was impossible
because seeing isn't always enough for belief.

After a Long Winter

Snowmelt sounds like applause
slapping the flooded dooryards.
From the sky, each gull cries
a child's laughter. The river
cheers its own weight,
having recently become
not just one thing, but many.

Beach Houses in Snow

There is so much weight
it covers memory.
Scentless sun
snow like soap
shuttered shingles and their
dim interiors. Bereft?
Even the sand beneath is numb.
I imagine people
emerging out of the salt spray.
That I've had children
has nothing to do with me
or bravery.
I seek any living thing,
find the only motion is waves.
What has frozen over
merely seems like permanence
but could be chance
the way wind can carry something
whether it wants to go or not.

My Son Says

*Soon the moon
will display the flashing lights
of human disturbance,
experimental explosions
we will see from Earth.*

I'm trying to articulate
how the full moon's light
on snow makes it clear
we are living on a planet,
our heads and roofs jutting out into space but

storms take my words away
on a wind that's traveled
here from everywhere else.
It's expensive to love
when it's so often a risk.

What news doesn't enrage us?
That we blunder on
into this misted-over violence
startles just when
we were feeling so swaddled.

His excitement baffles me.
I'm resistant to change, progress.
I love the moon as if it was a parent –
and see it that way –
constant, immortal.

*Nothing would make me enjoy
that sight* I say,
and then I wonder if
I've already sent him away
to his own planet

where he can hover
over, a pinprick of light
I can track from down here
among the trees and birds
who've never counted on me.

Proof

They've hired a body language expert
to interpret my dreams
of other women handing me their sickly babies
and being able to nurse again.
In pity, my breasts recall the twinge and spurt
but I wake up dry.

They've hired a handwriting expert
to analyze the cuneiform
on the walls of my uterus.
My son said he saw wolves in there.
I don't imagine this was a good experience.
I visualize it cut out and discarded.

My daughter asked if I could still give her a sister.
That she feels this as something missing saddens me.
What's worse, at twelve, she's begun
to ask me why her hips are so narrow.

For proof that women are real
I look at Tintoretto's Origin of the Milky Way.
Juno's breast milk sprays past baby Hercules –
denies him immortality –
as if its propulsion is what rockets her to the heavens,
keeps her painted flesh suspended there.

Oh, but the stars her milk births,
and the lilies of the earth
experts agree were cut from the canvas –
as if proof of their existence
depends upon their disappearance.

Journey to the Underworld

Her son's going through grungy glass doors.
They need renovation like the people
who wander beyond them.
Men half asleep in depression or addiction,
teenage girls carrying funhouse mirrors.

He stops at the sound only he can hear –
a whispering voice behind him, jerks his head around.
Sometimes it screams, he says, and she can't believe it.

He's seeing a shadowy figure. Last night
he threw a spoon at it. He's terrified.
They're going to find the source, interview him again
in the green plastic chairs, take away his shoelaces.

The TV in the lobby plays a marathon of home
improvement shows. On the couch, a man tucks his
chin to his chest and crosses his boots on the cushion.
Awkward children jump and grunt.

At the intake exam, his mother sobs intermittently.
I just want him to be normal again.
Her son looks on in sympathy. He's resigned, gives up
his phone. There are conditions.
No one knows how long he will stay.
The shatter-proof windows lock on the outside.

She turns to look back at him before
the doors double lock. It happens as she expects.
The keys she thought she had, leak
like music from her eyes.

Cape Cod, Massachusetts

The ocean borders this thin strip of bony arm.
Ospreys work the currents of sky, dive
the vortex into its dim dime shine.
What is overarching, deeper, higher,
the raptors' sleek bodies steal,
slip their feathers between breezes,
make this vast world small.
Their solitary journey south starts suddenly,
over the Straits of Florida to South America
and back again where they mate for life.
Nests high atop man-made boxes survey
Wychmere Harbor's ruffled water, patterned with boats
whose masts clang with metal sea sound.
One waits, the other vaults into the air and, screeching,
searches the shift of layered fathoms, the great metallic
sheen, and the black jutting jetty,
a backbone dividing the safe from the rough.

A transitory gray overhead as on our wedding day
where all our guests believed in promises…
But down in the matter of the poet's mind,
like a tattoo pen's staccato spirals,
fear stitches its itchy thread.
Our child, that scratched up gem – each day readies
to migrate away from the magnetic light of home.

A Harp Seal

A baby is like spring no matter when it's born –
never mind tender grass and resilient crocus; think how
ice on the river sends out its polygon rafts.
Water courses underneath like shadows,
like spirits of everything that has ever lived.

I find the harp seal just when I give up my search,
where the ice is still thick enough for this slick amoeba.
Watch how the head and tail fins lift
with love toward the very sun that dismantles its stage,
as if pulled by the strings of an invisible puppeteer.

How like my daughter dancing, all
springing legs and shaking hair.
A year past newborn, she knows
what she loves and how to show it.
I wish for her a floor and legs
that adapt if the boards melt away,
and if she's alone that she chose it that way.

Cold-Blooded

The tiny frog dipped in white yogurt
hopped through the library
showed its pattern of thought.
My daughter has been out all night
on her own at age nine,
this is concerning but I come back
to the home where we are staying
to take a picture of their turtle
only to find she had eaten him
shell and all except the face.
Then she wanted to eat a giant
white grub that wriggled
like a muscled tongue
under the dull edge of the butter knife.
The owners came home and asked
Who told you you could eat turtle?
We were outside now amidst
large rock formations.
The one that fit my body
rocked like a rocking chair.

My Daughter Asks:
What happened the first time it rained?

Arid gasp of sun-dusted curtains,
oh, to be a willow in this wind

with reedy limbs that brush and sway
as if fingers have just strummed them.

Instead I hear the wave-slapped gray bulk of hull
and doves moan in a parody of mourning.

We have no language for what befalls us:
everything cloaked in white chiffon

begins to dot darker,
stains every thirsty thing.

A punch of purple crocus
the bravest of babies,

forsythia blossoms vibrate
like a blur of bees' breath,

daffodils moody crowns
dip to the dewed grass,

and we in our hot bed of frustration
can't help but hear each pinprick of isolation

tap the glass like our fear of it ending
of something else coming

a low rumble just under our hearing
sensed as an increasing ache

until it bursts then quiets.
And now we know what that was –

we've spindled up through that slaking,
tendrils that curl and weave our flesh

into quenched organs
that flower helplessly into fruit.

What I Love About Dreams

Their open corridors narrow
to muddy birth canals
until I find myself flung up
to hover in a sudden sky then skim
upon eddies and whirlwinds,
down a sea of vortices.

Their town center has a waterfall
only the brave have navigated.
It begins at the church hill
winds through town, down
through the boulders' elephant heads
to the mobile homes' asphalt.

Their landmarks recur – a past home
or church, theater, or school –
but the architect has put an ocean in the basement.
It's okay, I like it better this way
with secret slides and doors that have never been,
but have always been open.

Theirs is the lodgement of memory forgotten
bringing back the glint of green from those glass
marbles we'd thumb down
the channels of exposed oak roots,
click the tiny globes of each of our worlds
against each other, as if they were the only reality.

The Mystery of Footprints

At the top of a mountain
there is a blue-green lake,
so clear you can see all
the way to the bottom
where boulders are spotted
with some dream lichen –
cold water and children
on the opposite shore
tossing in stones.
At my feet a mystery:
tiny tracks in the snow.
What animal made them?
How did I get –

Here, my son wakes me.
I don't want to help him.
He's nervous. He's had a nightmare,
can't even go back
to bed on his own.
I take him there, trying to hold on
to the feeling of that delicious water.
I ask him about his bad dream;

he tells me robbers came in
and stole me away from him.
I share my dream
to soothe him. He says 'night
before I'm finished. The mystery
of footprints still unsolved.

At the Dream Museum

maybe they knew my young daughter and son
would visit today

so they've covered the glass coffin
with a tasseled brocade

if you lift it you can witness
a rape

a silicone woman
her open mouth hissing air

at the pressure of his knees
as he kneels on her chest

he covers her with his crab's body
spider-crawls up to her head

perpetually climbs her like a ladder
his face plastic and mottled

features made from small doll parts
a torso for a nose

skinny arms for hair
she's a doll herself

not much of her to see except
the hole between her legs

like the plastic babydoll I used to fill in the bathtub
and watch the water run out

my children hear it too
the breath escaping is not breath

but audible
even under glass and the heavy weight of art

Driving to Your Parents

On New Hampshire back roads –
a film reel that has replayed for ten years
the same landscape. Each building
an inanimate character.

The latest winter storm
brought that birch's white
elbows down through someone's roof
like a giant, sullen child.

Whose barn is it that crumbles beneath
snow's weight?
I've never seen a single soul near it.
I am amazed
it remains standing.

The children bicker in the back seat,
kick at each other
and ask the hard questions:
"Did Jesus really exist?" and,
"Who made these mittens?"

Horses stand still within their fences,
blankets on their backs, grazing or staring.
Someone fed them grain, painted the farm sign.

It occurs to me that I feel
angry on the return drive.
I don't know why
and I never expect it.

There's that tarpaper shack –
must be inhabited by an elderly man.
Though I've never seen him, in my mind
he is cold, alone and trying to light a fire.

Like someone asphyxiating,
the windows inhale against their plastic wrap.

Someone I Love Might Die

Everywhere I look there is something undone –
the mirror flashes a complex eye,
does not look back long.

Your hands glazed hard with swelling,
your yellowed body upon the bed is a stranger
without the candor of your open eyes –
a stranger even to you, who have become
accustomed to the body's betrayal.

There is the mercy of snowfall without one mar,
and the spine of the book we meant to give you
the prettiest one on the shelf, still unread.

And before that, how much time,
how many objects, gifts,
words, how to measure your pain,
your swallowed gall, your pent up bile?

Except to see it in the moon's shadowed side
visible tonight as it sags liver-lipped above the city,
its crescent like the blade of a scythe,
that, being human, I try to describe.

STARLAND

An epitaph seen on a headstone in a dream cemetery.
Is this where you went?
In my darkened bedroom one night when you were dying
I saw light through a squint of tears,

like a transmission winking out.
I thought I was seeing the exact moment
of your death. You lived for two more days.
Cars and people kept passing even after.

The fire in the trees not yet lit then
now sparks in the mists of mornings I can't grasp.
I can't hold in my vision
any scene on the verge of change,

any autumn meadow with horses' grazing heads.
Their placement is as random as if dropped
from somewhere high up; their backs, studded
with sunlit dew, seem to hover between

the slats in the fence that divides us.

Night Walk While You are Dying

The idea of night is black and still,
but house facades are burnished
bronze by a streetlamp,
and the air smells briefly of skunk.

Pale fog condenses
beneath a golden porch light
snapping on. "Night, Pa",
someone says as she leaves his door.

Car headlights slide up the black
grease of trees, ghosting them
apparition white. Shadows pounce
up and out, jump the walls of a house
beyond, and then the chiaroscuro is gone.

The tree is itself a shadow.
Something made. Charcoal branches
against a star-wet sky. A train blows
through, its interior grows from within –
each empty seat a movement.

The motion in an upstairs window –
a girl in red pajamas, wet hair
obscures her face as she turns
toward something unseen.

In another house a woman's back
recedes down a hallway, vanishes.

Veins in the asphalt like black blood.
Every bundle on the sidewalk hides a figure.
Every thing by some absence, transformed.

Amazing Story

A piano technician survived
the New York gas explosion,
the massive wood and steel
instruments fell benignly –
shielded his body from the weight
of five stories worth of debris.

The pianos flew in the air –
pianos were all around me.
They were literally on their side.
I was stuck in some
miraculous cocoon of pianos.

In my dream a blown off
burned and broken door
falls sideways in front of me,
leans against a tree.
I think of you, beloved
and how all of us
are thrown to chance:
gifts that can save us
if only we open them.

News of the Missing Girl

An image recurs: a yellow leaf
everyone thought would land
is condemned mid-fall
to the purgatory of a spider's web.
Palimpsest upon which the story's written.
Ink erased, inked, re-erased
until holes rub through
like the jeans of ill-used girls.
Deleted names of girls
mothers have pained into this world,
girls singled out daily
by some mad god's eye
cracking comfort
like the thinnest ice.
Even the dunnest sparrow
can be stalked as she moves
through browned marsh grass –
the tips shiver with minute explorations
until she's gone and everything
left behind is still here
keeping the vigil of revision.
Consider this kind of loss.

Midsummer Murder Suicide

Thunder drums the vellum sky.
The treetops serrated edge, incised,
like writing down to the wood
of the kitchen table where they ate.

A white moth bumbles through
the chain link, plaits the air.
The dragonfly alights, stays.
Spiderwebs soften the porch corners.

The annuals, leggier now than in May
the light somehow lighter
more seared with clarity and slanted shadow
like an etching left too long in acid.

Slice of pool blue,
tangerine slash of shade,
fiery lilies curl open, close,
like a hand that signals *shut up*.

Leaves like fish of the air
torn with bullet silver.
Cars with no one to drive them
abandoned in the driveway.

The news in the neighborhood.
Two helicopters circle.
A man who killed a woman is dead.
The curtains are all closed.

The porch light burns absurdly
through this eternal daylight.
Cryptic glyphs, each burned-out
blade of our doomed lawns.

I dreamed that

as we watched
the weatherman crush
his tin foil replica of a tornado,
you were trying to burn down
our house by wrapping the gas
fireplace with blankets
while our children slept upstairs.
"Don't fall asleep," you said,
as the air grew infernal.
I didn't wonder if I should leave you
but listened, and awoke, ablaze.

Can You Hear Me?

The quiet are listening,
hearing silence.

Nothing will happen today
or everything I fear might –
calamity or that redundant inertia.
What will it be?

A gong rings in the new year,
vibration slides over everything.
If I stay still, asleep or awake,
nothing can be provoked.

What is said about this?
I'm one of many?
I love those people who can lift up
even the most dying person,

make a day seem like
what it was meant for –
not this.

Perennial as Love

Goodbye green
ugly Hostas
transmuting down to brown
brittle paper-skin leaves.

Haggard stems stagger with heads like old soldiers,
reveal the veins in our own fractured armatures.
Underneath, our roots curl in on slumber
seek comfort against our stranger selves.

I can hear the door banging
even now, feel the stiff white
nubs of the old sofa better
than anything you said to me.

That's my fault.

Things that come back
are remembered:

the dogged delphiniums,
the fleeting peony bud covered in ants,
the first time
my body sobbed *I love you.*

Now I can't remember
the last time those words unfurled
or if they have simply packed up
and tucked in – dormant adornments –
practicing their gritty alchemy under dark soil.

Back of the Dance Class

Leave excellence to the dancers whose minds work
automatically – the way you might button a sweater.
Salsa free of thought. Feet rhythmic,
tethered to the balloon of their animal brain.

Leave it to others to remember the moves, your mind
has gone dreamy, seasons marked by the flicker
of blue screens. Forget the leaves,
there are millions left to fall. They will leave.

Only then can you feel the sky open to transparency,
and witness how winged things navigate in vees
or singularly, seemingly aimless, puppeted in the air
as if on a kite string, and you
the anchor, always dragging your iron feet.

Voice while Driving

My mouth does an Iggy Pop,
eyes sore from dripping wrinkle cream,
knees brittle, in and out.

The road will give you a sore back.
This is how it goes –
peering through the dark for the familiar
in other people's homes,
or the unexpected –
wondering if tonight's the night
you'll hit the bear that lumbers
straight out of your imagination
and into your headlights.
You think I won't turn this wheel
straight into the guardrail?

I'm a fanatic of songs that distract
me back to the moon of my childhood.
Like a fragrance it follows me,
appears slashed in half,
both as small and as large
as a floater in the aging eye.

The Poem She Never Wrote

Was born past midnight,
stood stopped in the freezing foyer
of a college friend's rented house,
looking out the sidelight windows
at the full moon that struck so hard
and thought: *I must be written
when she gets home.*

Instead she stayed out late
and forgot the connection
between the way the moon looked
and the glass through which she saw it –
antique and therefore warped
like memory or age.

And then she had papers to write
and graduation to attend
and a boyfriend to marry
and babies to birth.

But she never forgot the image
of that white moon through glass.

She thinks about it at night
before falling asleep,
what she had meant to do
all those years ago.
What had been so important
about the way the air froze
coming out of her mouth
and fogged the vision?

It's almost enough to stop her worries –
her growing-up children
asleep in their beds –
this poem that never was.

Winter River

In December the river runs alongside the road
and appears to be the same color as the road.

When snow is falling only branches stand between
your car, you, and the plunging depth of steel-

colored water, and you are coming from the sky,
or maybe you were meant to be someone else.

The Jar with the Dry Rim
– after a title by Rumi

It hasn't always been dry.
Once it had the kiss of a salty lip.
The jar had been opened
in a moment of need.
The design met the desire
of the opener. First, a hand,
damp with sweat and grimy
with garden dirt reached out
thought nothing of future want,
eventual need, swiveled
the metal lid after a brief effort.
The dry tongue and aching lung
tipped the glass jar to the sun
and water was like a meal, elemental,
like breaking the surface of water
after holding a breath for too long.
Now, its rim is dry, a vessel
awaiting the richness of refilling.

Acknowledgments

I am grateful to the editors of the following journals where these poems first appeared:

The Light Ekphrastic (August 2017): "Night Walk While You are Dying"; *Nixes Mate Review* (Summer 2017, online): "Accident", "The Jar with the Dry Rim"; *The Wild Word* (2017, May 23, online): "The Poem She Never Wrote", "Proof";
Nancy Drew Anthology, Silver Birch Press (2016, October): "Mystery"; *Local Nomad* (2016, January): "I dreamed that", "What I Love About Dreams", "STARLAND", "Painting", "At the Dream Museum";
Bluestem Magazine (Autumn 2015, online): "November"
Bluestem Magazine (March 2015): "The Beekeeper's Daughter"; *The Cafe Review* (Autumn 2014): "News of the Missing Girl"; *Off the Coast, Maine's International Poetry Journal* (Summer 2014): "Back of the Dance Class"; *Literary Mama* (January 2008, online): "The Mystery of Footprints"; *What is Home: An anthology of the Portsmouth Poet Laureate Project* (2007): "202 Bank Street, Harwich Port, Massachusetts"

About the Author

Jessica Purdy has lived in New England all her life and currently resides in Southern New Hampshire with her husband and two children. Having majored in both English and Studio Art at UNH, she feels drawn to the visual in both art and poetry. She has worked as an art teacher and a writing teacher. Currently, she teaches Poetry Workshops at Southern New Hampshire University. She holds an MFA in Creative Writing from Emerson College. In 2015, she was a featured reader at the Abroad Writers' Conference in Dublin, Ireland. Her poems have appeared in many journals, including *The Light Ekphrastic*, *The Wild Word*, *Nixes Mate Review*, Silver Birch Press "Beach and Pool Memories" Series and their "Nancy Drew Anthology", *Local Nomad*, *Bluestem Magazine*, *The Telephone Game*, *The Tower Journal*, *The Cafe Review*, *Off the Coast*, *The Foundling Review*, and *Flycatcher*. Her chapbook, *Learning the Names*, was published in 2015 by Finishing Line Press.

Nixes Mate Books features small-batch artisanal literature, created by writers that use all 26 letters of the alphabet and then some, honing their craft the time-honored way: one line at a time.

More Nixes Mate titles:
ON BROAD SOUND | Rusty Barnes
KINKY KEEPS THE HOUSE CLEAN | Mari Deweese
SQUALL LINE ON THE HORIZON | Pris Campbell
COMES TO THIS | Jeff Weddle
HITCHHIKING BEATITUDES | Michael McInnis
AIR & OTHER STORIES | Lauren Leja
WAITING FOR AN ANSWER | Heather Sullivan
A WORLD WHERE | Paul Brookes
MY SOUTHERN CHILDHOOD | Pris Campbell
THE WILLOW HOWL | Lisa Brognano
CAPP ROAD | Matt Borczon
NIXES MATE REVIEW ANTHOLOGY 2016/17

Forthcoming titles from Nixes Mate:
LUBBOCK ELECTRIC | Anne Elezabeth Pluto
JESUS IN THE GHOST ROOM | Rusty Barnes
HEART OF THE BROKEN WORLD | Jeff Weddle
SMOKEY OF THE MIGRAINES | Michael McInnis
SHE NEEDS THAT EDGE | Paul Brookes

nixesmate.pub/books

www.ingramcontent.com/pod-product-compliance
Lightning Source LLC
Chambersburg PA
CBHW052135010526
44113CB00036B/2269